OH! FOR THE LOVE OF OLD...

HOUSES THAT IS!

By

Sandy Black

515 South Flower Street, 18th and 19th Floors,

Los Angeles, California, 90071

ISBN: 978-1-917344-34-0

Library of Congress Number: 2022915634

You may visit her at her website: booksbysandyllc.com
and email: blackbrunson5@gmail.com

This book is a work of fiction. Names, characters, places are a product of the authors imagination.

Table Of Contents

Dedication:

In Memory of Kraig Alan Black, a loving son and brother and our beloved nephew, Bobbie Eugene Whitmill. We grieve their loss and celebrate their life. They will be missed.

Acknowledgements:

To the Kingery's for sharing their beautiful 'house' for the cover of "Oh! For the Love of Old…Houses That Is!" To: Laura for always being there to lift, listen and love- one book or ten.

Chapter One
The Magnificent House on Walnut

John Leonard came home earlier than normal. Usually, he had meetings at the Glass Company or the Bank and recently involved his work as the County Auditor. Often arrived too late to have dinner with the children and his wife, Suzi, but Miss Macey, the family house maid, always put a hot plate back so he would have a warm dinner.

Hearing the back door open, 'Kitty Augustus,' named after her master, jumped down from his napping place near the big quilting board located in the front sitting room and ran all the way through the parlor to greet his favorite person. Mr. Leonard stooped down, picked up his overweight buddy, scratched his ears and put him back down. At that time, he heard Ms. Suzi coming through the kitchen. "John, what's the matter? We're home so early. Is there something wrong at the Bank or The Glass Factory?" He shrugged and smiled as a couple of the children wrapped themselves around his legs. "I'm not sure. I got a message today from a carrier stating one of the influential stockholders wanted to stop by the house to discuss something in private."

She walked toward him, laid her head on his chest and said, "Oh dear! You don't think."

'Kitty Augustus' decided to go upstairs where his friend, 'Kitty Spike' was no doubt in the nursery sleeping under a crib or on a bed listening for the new babies who had to be fed more often. He was not all that fond of the noise that the rambunctious children made when they came home from school. 'Kitty Spike,' an orange, fluffy sort who was always being picked up and toted around the house and dropped at will, loved the nursery and appointed himself the house alarm when the nurse had stepped out. She knew when he started a loud screech noise that one of the babies was awake and needed attention. Both felines determined the conversation downstairs in the library office might be of the serious kind.

John said, "Suzi, let us not get overly excited. When we do, it overflows upon our children and staff. It could be to discuss the leases on our farmland or those City lots we own. He could be putting his name in for a political assignment. The word is out that I will not seek re-election for City Council. I must devote the bulk of my time to the Auditor position if I am to do it right. My plate is too full now. So, let's not panic. I'll be in the library office for a while. I have some Glass Company business to shore up."

An hour or so later, Ms. Suzi stuck her head into the library and said, "I have a plan. You just need to trust me. What time will he be here?" He replied, "Friday at 1:00 o'clock." She smiled her infectious smile and said, "Perfect," and quietly closed the library door.

'Kitty Augustus' and 'Kitty Spike' knew something was up. Kitty Augustus' said, "We have to stay close and be ready to help however we can."

"Byron, Byron, come quick!" "Yes, Mam". "I want you to hand carry, and I mean HAND CARRY, these eight invitations today. I want you to wait until they open them so you can report back - hear?" "Yesum." "Well, hurry on!"

Byron, a middle-aged, freed slave, lived and worked for the house on Walnut. His wife, Clemma, was also free and was the full house maid. She loved her job of taking care of the babies on the second floor. He told her he was on a mission and would return as soon as he could.

The delicately written invitation on the personal note of rose pattern Ms. Suzi had designed especially for these types of occasions read:

You are cordially invited to attend the 'first' planning meeting of the proposed Hartford Library.

Friday, 1:00 pm

Tea and scones will be served.

We will be joined by Miss Margaret Sole', who will share her vast knowledge of Library development. Mrs. Suzi Leonard

Friday Morning

The stately house on Walnut became a beehive of activity. Fresh wood at each fireplace, beautiful fall flowers in various vases in the house, with a special one on the dining room table. China tea pots, matching cups and saucers shined to perfection. Tiny, rose bud trimmed napkins. The finest lace tablecloth and polished silverware made the table a welcome site. The large family-size dining room table sat near the only bathroom, which was spotless to include a new rug and a bouquet of rose petals. Ladies, no doubt, would enjoy a tour at the close of their meeting.

Mr. George Wayford and John Leonard would find a welcoming fire in the library fireplace and a tray of hot tea and warm scones. He was thinking to himself that all the children were in school and that their sweet giggles might be welcome today.

'Kitty Augustus' lay near the bathroom, out of the way of the servants who were tending to Suzi Leonard's important guests. At 1:00 pm sharp, nine ladies were met and led to their seats at the beautifully decorated dining room table. Eight very animated ladies were introduced to their special guest speaker, and a discussion of the new Hartford Library made for some lively conversation. At times, nine ladies seemed to talk all at once. 'Kitty Augustus' told 'Kitty Spike,' "I think whatever plan Miss Suzi had in mind, well, it must be working."

Almost unnoticed, at 1:00 sharp, Mr. George Wayford rang the doorbell. Byron opened the door with a big, welcoming smile, and John Leonard escorted him to the library. John apologized for not knowing his wife would be entertaining a group of ladies who were dedicated to seeing a much-needed library for the town's children. Hopefully, it is located right in the middle of town for all to enjoy.

In the library office, the two men chatted small - talk mostly - about the state of the county's political direction while enjoying hot tea and scones. The group down the hall sounded as though they were plotting for a positive vote at the upcoming City Council meeting, where all would be in attendance to state their case for the need for a Hartford Library.

Mr. Wayword sat his cup down and casually said, "John, you certainly have a magnificent house here. A separate kitchen outside would be my wife's dream, along with the bathroom and that unbelievable tub. imagine your house will be the talk of the town when these ladies get done with their tour." John smiled and said, "Thank you, Sir."

'Kitty Augustus,' a green-eyed, black ball of fur, said to 'Kitty Spike.' "They have been in the library long enough. These ladies sound like their chattering is more about this house, which means they want to take 'the tour.'

"Just curious, John, have you heard anything about the Underground Railroad? Has it that there are people who are hiding slaves and giving them safe journeys to the North? There is some KKK. movement to include going to Sunday church services and openly threatening those who might be harboring slaves. Even burning their houses and everything in it to the ground."

John spoke very softly. "George, I am a stockholder like you and Director of the State Bank, own a bit of farmland and, over the course of a month, attend a host of meetings. I think if there was an active Underground Railroad, I would have heard something, even if it were just gossip. But, if anything comes up in any meetings, including in my Auditor briefings, I will personally let you know." Mr. George Warford seemed more relaxed and even laughed at all the noise coming from the dining room. He said he would go to the restroom, but walking through a tea party with eleven women and two cats might not be received well!"

John ushered Mr. George Warford to the front door, and he bowed to the ladies who were gathering their things for their exit. The official Library Committee was adjourned. The resident cat, who had been napping on the big red bathroom rug, looked around at the meticulously designed House on Walnut and remarked, "You sure pulled off a good one, my friend." The House on Walnut looked at his feline friend and said, "Not to worry, 'Kitty Augustus,' I'm built so sound you can't hear a thing below the first floor - know what I mean!"

John Leonard looked at his wife and said, "I think I need something a little stronger to drink than what is in that china tea pot. His wife, who had just said goodbye to her last guest, walked over to her husband's side and got a big, well-deserved hug. Everyone, including the resident cats and the servants, gave a big sigh of relief.

There is often a price for freedom.

The Underground Railroad officially ended around 1863

Chapter Two
THOSE OLD SODDIES!

Amanda was watching her twelve-year-old brother, Kale and 'Kitty Eustace', the very opinionated family cat, romping through the thickly rooted prairie grass. Had made camp in Nebraska to rest a few days before heading out to San Francisco. Stood impatiently waiting on her parents, Marcus and Edith Stone, who seemed to be at odds and in deep discussion off and on these past few weeks. Always walked away from camp to talk out of their children's ear shot. Amanda's father raised his voice, which was very unusual for him. Kitty Eustace' came running up and said, "What is it with those two? I heard Mr. Marcus talking about homesteading. What's that?" Amanda said, "It doesn't concern us, 'Kitty Eustace' cause we are going to San Francisco! I have been sewing my "coming out" dress ever since we left our home in Virginia. Know there are so many rich families already there, and who knows, I may even marry a banker or a doctor, and I will have my own house."

Later that day, the family once again gathered around a make-shift table and a glowing fire. Beans flavored with a little salt pork were cooked most of the day, and biscuits with homemade strawberry jam were brought from 'back home.' Mr. Marcus told Kale to gather enough sticks for the fire to last all night, and Amanda's mother, Edith, told her they would wash some clothes in the morning in the purest water they had ever seen. Talk, Amanda thought.

The next morning, Amanda spoke up. "Mother, when are we leaving? Aunt Pid and Uncle Buck should be here within the week with the next caravan. Aunt Pid is bringing my ribbons to finish my dress."

Edith Stone looked at her husband and said, "I think it is time we had a talk!" She continued, "It seems your father, Uncle Buck, Reverend Waters and others have been presented with an opportunity." 'Kitty Eustace' stopped cleaning his whiskers and jumped up beside Amanda to make sure he heard the 'scoop.' He had felt something was coming. From the looks on Miss Edith's face, something was. frowned upon and said, "What opportunity, father?"

"Everyone gather around, please, and don't say anything until I am done." Mr. Marcus began, "We have an opportunity to pay a small registering fee to do what they call 'Homestead,' which is a parcel of land right here. We work the land, live on the land, develop it, and then, after five years, the land will be ours. We are not squatters. We are settlers who can become land owners under a new "Homestead Act" just signed by President Abraham Lincoln.

Amanda looked at Kale in disbelief. Mother, what about my debut in San Francisco? My new dress? Will we live? There are no trees, nothing but dumb old land with a bunch of prairie grass. Who would want this worthless land anyway? Do you talk to him? Looked down at 'Kitty Eustace' and asked, "What will we do? We have no friends, no house, no school, no church, NOTHING!" Kales' father walked up to see sad faces and angry and disappointed children. "I know you and your sister are young and do not understand all this, but we have no money. Everything we have is in our wagon, and it got us this far. Uncle Buck has learned how we can build houses without any money. As you can see, we have little to no trees." "What are we gonna do, father? With a swollen face from so much crying, her mother and Kale pulled closer to hear the plan.

"We will build our first prairie home called a 'sod house.' Amanda said, "A WHAT? O.H. Good Gosh!!" Her father softly spoke, "First, let's remember something very important. By agreeing to farm these 160 acres, we will be getting more than just getting free land. We will be helping to develop America across the west. Aunt Pid, Uncle Buck, and others will be staying with us, and they are bringing fifteen committed families with them. We know how to farm and raise cattle and also, let's not forget, we left a farm we did not own, and it was worn out. We needed a new start. This is our opportunity to that new life."

Amanda's Mother, Edith, spoke up for the first time. "I know this area is almost treeless, and we cannot build a cabin right now. Be assured in the future, we will build one when those coming from the east bring the necessary supplies. But remember, the ground beneath us is ours. There have been reports by other settlers that they are having success with the 'sod houses.' AND that is what we and others are going to build. WE ARE GOING TO LIVE IN A DIRT HOUSE?" Amanda went screaming off to the covered wagon, where a beautiful dress hung neatly in the back, closely followed by Kitty Eustace. No opinions were offered.

Kale had been quietly studying the situation. "Maybe building a dirt house might be fun, and I offered to help. Nearly thirteen, he would assist the others in a big way. Edith decided she best try to console her very unhappy daughter. She had already decided her life was all but over.

Building the "soddy" house

'Kitty Eustace' was observing the activity. "Making bricks out of grass. Uncle buck must be drinkin' something! I see long, tall grass. Don't look to me like you could plant anything, much less build a house. Mr. Stone is hitching up the horses. Said he had to break up the soil after the big rain. The sod cutters who are immigrating here will be coming in on one of the caravans. They originally came from another country and knew how to make strips of sod and then cut them into bricks with an ax. Stone and others will stack the ' bricks' into walls. Then roofs will be formed with twigs, hay and covered with thick sod bricks as well. "Who would have thought!"

Aunt Pid and Miss Edith were talking about how lucky they were to have a big hill on their acreage. Their sod houses will be built on the sides of the hill already dug out. Only the front and the roofs need to be completed. Mr. Yanasee, one of the sod cutters, said this would keep them warmer in winter but cooler in the very hot summers.

Time Passes on --Reality Sets IN!

"So much for a real house. room, four people, one feline - real luxury". 'Kitty Eustace,' he thought as he looked across six-foot-tall grass. Miss Edna is always worrying about the children getting lost and admonishes them to stay close to their 'soddie.' "Oh, not to worry, 'Kitty Eustice' to the rescue.

Amanda started writing in her notebook Aunt Pid, also a school teacher, brought her. She wrote: "Life is a big nowhere!". Everything, and I mean everything, is extreme. Summers are so hot, you can make hot tea. Then, without notice, a rainstorm will come through and wash the front of a farmer's soddie-built house away. , a tornado came roaring through and here we are, sitting against the hill in our sod house. No trees. Nothing to stop the massive wind.

The new sod house was sad for the children, but they knew over time, they would be a community and life would be good. "And that cat with all his opinions is something else!"

Another entry - January

Early on, father built a 'dugout.' Mother had a fit that she might have to live in a dark hole and would cease to live. It proved to be warmer and drier than our wagon. Especially since canvas has no protection at all from this wind. As promised, father built our soddie right in front of the dugout. Today, during another tornado warning, we pushed our cow, 'ole Buttercup" into the dugout and 'Kitty Eustace' kept an eye on her since it was not a field with room to wander. Kale sat with them since that was one of the safest places around and sang songs from the hymnal Reverend Snow had given him. He remarked, "Will this winter ever end?" I ask the same thing every day, as noted in this journal.

It is finally spring.

'Kitty Eustace' gave Kale his opinion, to be kept to himself, of course, that he thought Ms. Edna Stone and her husband chose their 160 acres very well. We have a flowing creek and several hills that 'sort of' keep the wind-down, and not to gossip now, I heard several railroad lines are being planned for this area. That will make Amanda quite happy. don't talk about that now since she seems content to write in her notebook." Kale agreed and remarked, "There is talk of a new school soon to be built, and Aunt Pid will be the first teacher. The little sod house grinned.

As promised, Mr. Stone completed the first sod house and put it right in front of the dugout, and as the months passed, he helped numerous other homesteaders settle into their 'soddie.' Kale said, "Mother is so creative. Beginning to look a lot like home. She and Aunt Pid and several new homesteaders help each other settle in. Our beds and tables are built right in the 'hill walls.' Mother loves wallpaper and drugs, some of which are out of her old trunk. Said that covering the walls helped to keep the mice out. Pallets are not very much fun to sleep on, but you can move them during the day. Think one of the funniest things 'Kitty Eustace' that she has done is to take handfuls of flower seeds and throw them on the roof! The little sod house said, "Who does that?" 'Kitty Eustace' laughed and shook his head." "Did you see all those sheets of white muslin hanging on the

14

ceiling? Sure has helped keep the dirt and water from coming down in your evening soup." Well, I try to keep the snake population down by shaking the life out of them. an aggravation no one needs to wake up and have in their beds." giggled 'Kitty Eustice.'

Another year passed. Dozens of immigrants moved to the prairie. "Listen up, everybody. The Inspector from Washington is coming," said Uncle Buck. "I think we will pass with flying colors. Already have our sod houses built in front of a dug out, and all within the six-month claim agreements. We are living here, crops planted over sixty acres, two cows alive and thriving, and soon to be three. Window sills and roofs are a blaze of color with all the beautiful wild flowers."

The little sod house thought, "And I am the first wild flower roof built in the community."

The family gathered for a moment of prayer. Uncle Buck said, "Some of our immigrant friends have not been so fortunate. Unwelcoming weather, accidents and sheer loneliness have taken their toll. Some have given up on a dream of owning their own piece of land and "went back home."

Amanda continued to write in her notebooks and eventually made it to San Francisco, where she became a writer and journalist. Her favorite subject was 'Life in a Soddie'. Her brother, Kale, continued to help new settlers and became the first church pastor with his wife, Kathryn. 'Kitty Eustice' can be seen most days rescuing the children lost in the tall reeds. The little sod house watches him and giggles with joy.

January 1, 1863

New Homesteaders continued to go west. There were Millions of homesteads were granted between 1862 and 1934. About 60 percent of those claims granted were abandoned.

Those immigrants with 'grit' - 157,600 of them successfully "proved up."

Although not free.

Chapter Three
Do You Live in a Tee Pee? Nope, I Live in a Wickiup!

As the sun began to rise across the vast Jacarilla Apache Indian Reservation, 'Kitty Cibique,' the elder cat of the tribe, who has experienced much of the Apache history - good and bad, was admiring the beautiful red valley and canyon below. He decided it was time to go visit his friends, 'Kitty Red Star' and 'Wiki,' his newest dwelling friend.

'Wiki' shouted, "Hey fellas, sure a lot of activity goin' on, huh! Don't you just love the Juniper trees, the Ponderosa pine they used for my frame and the tall reeds and thatched grass with mud on my outside? And listen to this!! Miss Sadie, the oldest member of all our elders, has accumulated enough buffalo hides to cover me just as soon as my mud dries and the hole in the top of me is sealed. The tribal women will be coming to help do the hide covering, and there is nothing better than Mother Earth for my floors."

'Kitty Red Star' looked on with amazement. "It is so exciting to see the door facing the east, so the first thing we see in the morning is the rising sun. Father Sun is one of the most revered of the native deities. We are so lucky to be able to live with you 'Wiki.' This is such a sacred home, built by Holy people. We will surely be blessed with wealth and good fortune." 'Wiki' said, you know our people move a lot on our vast reservation. We need to find good hunting and fishing grounds as well as small areas rich in our little gardens. This is a must for the women. But, no matter where we tear down and go, you will always have a place to call home with me.

"'Kitty Cibique,' I have been meaning to ask you something. Where did you get your name?" "Well, my father and our Master were part of the 'Cibecue' Apache Indian band, known as Jicarilla Apache and also called Pelonas. They were fierce guerilla fighters. Remember how they bravely fought the Commanchies in 1716, and that is when we were driven off our land. 1724, we again fought long and hard, but most of our men were lost in that battle, and our remaining family members were taken prisoner. Father died, and our family hid off and on in the trunk of a ponderosa pine log. Seven years for those in prison, the U.S. Army, in 1877, came in and re-settled the Jicarilla Apache on land in New Mexico."

'Wiki' smiled. "Wow, and we are still here! AND we have a new home - M.E., The neatest buffalo-covered Wickiup around."

'Wiki' and 'Kitty Cibeque' thanked Miss Sadie, the two elders and all new occupants for their beautiful work. We will live where less fighting and more living in peace prevails."

Today, the reservation spans 879,917 acres in North Central New Mexico. Dulce, New Mexico, is the sole Jacarillo Apache Indian community with a population of 3,258

Chapter Four
The Little Adobe House with Board-and-Batten Siding

Looking across the uncharted land at the five or so wagons and the children scammering to get dressed and ready for the day caravan drive towards their new home, William Flake asked his wife, Lucy, if she had enough germade, the hot cereal for a few more children. He felt some looked very thin and sickly. Said, "Of course."

Lucy looked at her, deep in thought, husband and asked, "William, do you feel the cattle ranch on Silver Creek will be a better home for our children and those families following us than the land near the Little Colorado River settlement?" "That's a good and valid question, Lucy. I can tell you that ever since Brigham Young called us to serve the church, we have been searching for the right land. Other family members and I made our trip to Utah to sell our wool and buy some cattle. We came across Apostle Erastus Snows' carriage." "Who is he?" Lucy asked. "Turns out, he is a Mormon leader who was assigned by Brigham Young to direct the colonization efforts in Arizona. In 1878, he had already located the site area for the new Mormon town.

Continuing on, William told Lucy that for several days on that trip, he and the group spent several days discussing the plans for colonization and our calling by Brigham Young. Asked if he could visit the newly purchased Stinson Ranch. After our visit, he spoke confidentially to me about how impressed he was with what we had already accomplished. He then suggested we combine our efforts and make the town near the new farm site. Told him the land had come with a 4-room sun-dried, adobe house covered with board-and-batten siding. We agreed there was a large enough area for building larger homes, a church, a bank and a school as the town grew. It was then decided Snowflake was a perfect name for a town.

Lucy looked at her husband and smiled. "You know I will make every effort to help you succeed in your effort, and I will make a home wherever your calling leads us." "What about Penelope and the children?" William turned around and firmly said, "What about her?" "She and our twenty children will be going to the farm with us." "But, William, Arizona has a law against polygamy, and Penelope does not want to leave her family in Utah, Lucy tried to explain.

About that time, a sleepy-eyed, garden-variety cat named 'Kitty Thaddeus strolled in with two little boys. Named after Willam's son, Thaddeus, the self-appointed bodyguard was most interested in the new batch of cereal and warm milk Miss Lucy had cooking. The older children were already tending to milking the cows, getting wagons ready to roll and putting out campfires.

William said, "We will discuss this later."

The little adobe house in Silver Creek Valley was small but welcoming. This is not just for the Flake family but also for hundreds of visitors who might come through with a need over time. Lucy's hospitality and William Flakes' growing reputation that he was someone who bought ranches and turned them into towns. Often, they bought properties in Navajo and Apache Counties and then resold them to Mormon settlers at no profit later. Initial settlers were growing, and new families were coming in. One of those families helped in harvesting the crops. There was enough food to go around.

Jessie N. Smith, his five wives and forty-four children moved in 1870 to SnowFlake after Brigham Young called Jessie into service. He served as president of the Eastern Arizona Stake and later the SnowFlake Stake. Many new residents were pioneers of irrigation, and some, like Jessie Smith, learned how to utilize the water and share that knowledge. Towns flourished. Three crops of alfalfa were raised in a season, and numerous bushes of oats and wheat were harvested. Of the first things done by Lucy Flake and other wives was to plant peach, plum and apple trees. Trees were abundant over time as well. During those years, many pies were made and served at the little adobe house with Board-and-batten siding.

Unfortunately, things aren't always as one thinks it will or should be.

Many Mormons were of the mind that polygamous marriages performed in Utah could not be persecuted in Arizona. , they were wrong, and many were sent to prison for up to three years. Many fled to Mexico, and their wives went underground to Utah.

In December 1884, William J. Flake was arrested. He was sentenced to six months in prison at Yuma Territorial Prison plus a $500 fine for practicing polygamy.

The manifesto renouncing polygamy was issued in 1890.

William J. Flake never answered is first wife Lucy's question about Penelope. William continued to be married to both wives until their deaths, fathered eleven sons and 9 daughters and ignored the Edmunds Act of 1884 even though he was not allowed to vote, hold public office or serve on juries.

Jesse N. Smith left Snowflake in 1885. A move to Mexico was a way to avoid prosecution. Mormon towns in Mexico were prosperous. Jessie Smith died in Dubl'an in 1912.

Chapter Five
The Houses That Burned For Liberty

Robert Hemings, a fourteen-year-old enslaved servent who lived and worked to care for Thomas Jefferson at the aptly named Independence House, looked down at his sleeping companion, 'Kitty Liberty,' and said, "You best get up and movin'. Mr. Jefferson gotta go to his meetings of the Second Continental Congress. This is gonna be an important day for maybe signing the Declaration of Independence."

Looking rather sleepy-eyed since Mr. Jefferson wrote his draft all day and night, he said, "If you want my opinion, Mr. "Bob," the colonists are doin' the right thing. Big ole British King George, whatever number he is, has no business coming to America and ruining the colonists' lives. They are forced to move all the way near the Appalachians, have no say in their own self-government, pay enormous taxes 'to the King,' and are forced to house and feed the British Army with no pay. He puts restrictions on *everything they do!* If this Declaration of Independence does not work, then we need to give him a good 'whoopin'. Now that's just my opinion, you know."

The obedient slave who takes care of the "Independence House" and is much wiser than his years said, "I don't have much learnin', and so I just listen to Mr. Thomas Jefferson and the others talk about 'things.' heard him talk'in out loud to his self, and he said The Declaration of Independence was gonna be written so they could explain that **all** the colonists had a right to a revolution and Congress had to prove the legitimacy of the cause. He told Mr. John Hart that he hoped the world would rally around us, and he felt they needed to announce the creation of a new country."

'Kitty Liberty' said, "Wow, what a Patriot."

The days and months ahead.

Jefferson wrote with pride, 'His expression of the American mind," and with that came the Agreement of complete secrecy to protect the cause of liberty and for their own secrecy. He did not expect or like that Congress took his draft of the Declaration of Independence and "mangled" it. Kitty Liberty' thought, "Maybe that is why they call it a draft." Ultimately, everyone agreed we ought to be a free and independent state!

The 56 signers of the Declaration of Independence 'mutually pledged to each other their lives, their fortunes and their sacred honor." The Declaration was presented and rejected by the King. Even the Olive Branch Petitiion was not only rejected but caused the King to declare the colonies to be in open rebellion. Made his own Proclamation 'for Supporting Rebellion and Sedition.' He even hired thousands of mercenaries to assist the British troops, already in America in crushing the rebellion. They were very disciplined and had martial prowess.

The Revolutionary War lasted eight years because King George III refused to surrender to the colonies.

Those who served in Secrecy protected the cause of Liberty and joined the fight against tyranny.

Many colonists believed they should use non-violent means to protest all the British abuses. When 56 brave, soft-spoken men of means signed the Declaration of Independence, they did so, well knowing that the penalty would be death if captured.

John Hart lived on Sourwood mountain. The gently sloping hillside served as a place of respite for the American Army, who once camped and drank from the old Spring. "Honest John" owned cattle, sheep, horses, swine and four slaves. His wife was very ill, and the British tore through their farm where they lived and worked with their thirteen children. They were forced to flee for their lives. John escaped for nearly two years, living in the forests and caves. He returned to find his Gristmill and fields were laid to waste, children were scattered, and his wife, Deborah, had died. He was the 13th delegate to put his signature on the Declaration of Independence.

Thomas Stone was an American founding father, planter, politician and lawyer. He worked on the committee that formed the Articles of Confederation in 1777 and was a big promoter of anti-British policies. He owned a 442-acre plantation called Habre de Venture, and as the Maryland signer of the Declaration of Independence, he willingly made a decision that would cost him his property. April 1776, he stated, "You know my heart wishes for peace upon terms of security and justice to America. But, anything, including war is preferred to a surrender of our rights.

Chapter Six
It's Not Just A Drink, It's a Livin'!

"Man, that's high-proof stuff! Thanks to Mom. They're try'in to make us pay taxes on our own moonshine. Can you just believe that 'Kitty Shiner'? Didn't get them into this war, and now they want us to pay for all those dang debts, grumbled Ebonizer Small, a third-generation farmer and unknown to most, the head of a 'moonshine makin' family. 'Kitty Shiner,' also highly agitated, said, "Heck Eb, we just went through this with the Brits, and now they got this fancy, dancy 1862 Revenue Act! Revenue for who? We ain't havin' it. Are we E.B.?"

"No way. Now, the farmers around here are hearing the government declaring moonshine to be a 'danger' to our health. E.B. continued, they are pushin' this kind of garbage, alright. It's a bigger danger to our pocketbooks."

'Kitty Shiner' asked, "E.B., your Pa and Granpa have their own recipes for our moonshine. Do you know it?" E.B. quietly said, "Stillers here in Tennessee know we make 'our own' moonshine from a recipe that is older than dirt! One thing we all know for sure is we have to grow good corn and rye. Ole' Smokey Moonshiners keep their mouths shut, keep a low profile and above all else, it is the unwritten word that our secret ingredient is never, ever spoken out loud."

'Kitty Shiner' said, "I think we all know we would not even have a business if it weren't for Mama. She chose this desolate piece of land and exactly where Lily, our old farmhouse, was to be built down a lane and a heavy, fancy lookin' iron fence. People thought (and we have never told anyone any different) Mama was from the east 'cause she could read and write and had lots of books about all sorts of 'stuff.' Actually, Mama is known as the community Beekeeper. makes hundreds of jars of honey, and when she sets up her "HOME MADE HONEY" sign at the edge of the roads, cars from all over come to buy." Her customers even saved fruit jars since they are repeat customers, and most people don't know that our house, Lily, hides one of the biggest moonshine makin' Stills in Tennessee. Mama tends to makin' sure every recipe step is followed, and the place is spiffy clean. O.H.! By the way, Mama didn't come from the east. She came from a long line of respected moonshiners in Kentucky. did good!"

'Kitty Shiner' laughed out loud. "Mama's customers (honey or?)return the empty fruit jars. Can see why she complains about the new taxes on everything we do. She's the one who pays the taxes. Loved it when she designed our Still behind that 'fake wall' that looks like ceiling-to-floor bookshelves. I never asked Lily if Mama had read all those books on the shelves. On the backside of the staircase leading outside to a shed. 'shed' is totally surrounded by white beehives. Mama says, "We don't need a gun for 'Still lookers.' The Queen bee will take care of the Still." **The Queen bee and Mama are best friends, according to Lily.**

'Kitty Shiner' looked at his friend and said, "Eb, it looks like a good crop this year. Honey, Corn, Rye and ..."**SHHHHHH, you best remember what Mama said. "Keep your mouth shut and your head down!"**

'Kitty Shiner' quietly said, "Yes, Sir!"

Chapter Seven
Am I Gonna Live All the Way Back There?

Sundays were always hectic at the Mines farm. This day was more than just a Sunday School and church day. 'Kitty Fragilistic' was going around all bedrooms to make sure someone did not slip back under the covers. Ms. Clara Mines yelled up the stairs, "Everyone, make sure you have your Bibles. Girls, don't forget your sheet music for your special song." Teddy frowned, "Why do I have to go to church anyway? He does talk about where we are going if we aren't good. I can hear that right here at home." 'Kitty Fragilistic' came running down the stairs expecting to see Teddy either get a swat on the hiny butt or get a sermon before the real sermon was given later by his brother, Reverend Carl Mines. Teddy skirted through it all since this Sunday was not an ordinary Sunday.

"Hurry up, let's get the dishes readied up, the pies on the sideboard to finish cooling, the noodles drying on the table top for quickly dropping into the hot chicken broth as soon as we return from church. Ginny, bring down two cans of canned green beans and corn from the canning closet."

"What's all the ruckus about anyway?" Ruby asked. She had received no mail from Johney, her intended for weeks. From the Army bases was far too slow for her, and her interest was not in setting the big dining room table for dinner. Well, we have not told any of you because we thought we would have more details to share.

Seems Inez will be arriving home with a surprise all the way from California on a Greyhound bus today and should arrive mid-afternoon. have heard so little since she left to bury her husband in Tulare." "Can't we just stay home from church?" someone yelled from the front room. Mr. G. looked around and said, "NO, get in the car, or we will be late, and stop that talking." The car went down the long lane with the big elms all lined up like soldiers on both sides waiting to salute.

'Kitty Fragilistic' took off to the barn. Cleaning up the milk tin from the morning milking was a favorite thing to do, and a nap in the quiet of the hay made for a good Sunday. Opposum had just had a litter of tiny critters, and it was fun to watch them squirm. Makes one wonder how Miss Clara managed fourteen, including the twins, all those years. Had a funny feeling that "things were about to change".

Most Mines boys were in the armed services and away from home. The remaining family members gathered at the homeplace way back off the lane, waiting on their oldest sister, Inez. For a few winter months when the trees were barren, no one could see the house nestled among several kinds of fruit trees, the massive grape harbor, fencing covered on end with blackberries and raspberries waiting to be canned and later made into pies. It was the main 'decoration' around the outhouse. Many a hot rhubarb crisp and strawberry/rhubarb pie graced the Mines table from those stalks that grew wild. Such a large family required 365 days a year and a labor of love to maintain such a 'working' farm. It was very difficult with the boys all away at war, including Junior, Clara's baby, who joined at eighteen years of age.

Bobbie yelled, "There is a car coming down the road, and I think it is going to turn down the lane." Everyone came running out the door to see what surprise was to come out of the car with Inez. The car stopped, and Inez stepped out, holding a big blanket in her arms. Walked up to her parents and pulled off the blanket. Kitty Fragilistic' looked on and, like everyone else, didn't make a sound. Ginny said, "What is it?"

All of a sudden, a little scrawny, dark and curly-headed, brown-eyed girl looked around and saw Clara and Mr. G Hines and said, "Hi, Granny and Grandad, I haven't seen you in a long time!" The entire Mines family roared with laughter. The love bug had bitten them all. Most of all, it was Grandad Mines who named the little girl with a long name 'Andy'. Did not take her long to scoot 'Kitty Fragilistic' up in her arms, and thus changed a lot of lives forever. The strange feeling was a good one.

The story goes that Inez had gone to California to bury her husband, who died from a gunshot wound. During that time, it was revealed he had a niece who had been placed up for adoption in an orphanage due to severe family hardship. When all was said and done, the Greyhound bus left with Inez and a little girl with a long name headed for a new home in Indiana.

'Andy' and 'Kitty Fragilistic' made an immediate impact. Didn't look or act like any of the children nor the exploding Mines grandchildren that were coming very quickly. Blue-eyed, fair-skinned and knew when to not talk unless spoken to, a rambunctious, spontaneous, never stopped talking nor sat still a moment (even in church). Quickly learned to climb every tree, milk a cow, churn butter, pluck chickens, snap peas and beans, and pick strawberries without stepping on the precious patches which might be in various stages of ripeness. 'thought' she could drive a tractor. That turned out to be a bone of contention with Granny. It was felt that her 90 lbs might be better suited to learning sewing and embroidery and memorizing some Bible verses. Learned to drive a tractor on Grandad's lap and got proficient after knocking a fence or gate down as part of the learning curve. Kitty Fragilistic' could be found on the front seat of the 'Ole Farmall tractor, sitting between 'Grandad' and 'Andy.' She never learned to embroider or sew a stitch, but she got a white bible from Miss Owens, her Sunday School teacher, for memorizing everything from the Psalms, Beatitudes and others first in class. Grandad took her for a small ice cream cone and enjoyed bragging rights.

"What's that thing, Granny?" Andy asked. Oh, it's a bed pan, and your bed is called a feather tic 'cause it is full of duck feathers." Granny replied. You sit on that thing?" "Well, only at night. we go outside to the outhouse during the day." "Oh, okay."

The Outhouse - a disaster.

The rooster was making sure everyone knew it was time to get up. Was making her usual biscuits and huge iron skillet of milk gravy with ham and eggs. smell creeped up the stairway and no alarm clock was needed. day had begun.

Granny gave everyone their list of morning chores. "Andy, go to the outhouse, and when you are done, take this wire basket and gather the eggs. Seemed easier than filling the big iron bucket full of water for scalding chickens later.

"Help, Help me!!

Grandad came running around the end of the chicken house just as a big hen decided this new little singing chatterbox was a threat to her brood and in no way was going to let her stick her little bony hand under her to get eggs. Before she got a thorough flogging, Grandad came to the rescue. Andy and 'Kitty Fragilistic' carried the egg basket carefully to the house. Kitty Fragilistic' grinned at the house at the end of the lane and said, "This is one Granny Mines might not need to know about." His friend replied, "Yup, we sure didn't know what was comin' out of that blanket, but she has brought life into me, you and the entire Mines family. Some days, I am not sure who is teaching who."

Andy lived with her grandparents while Inez worked in the tire factory for the war effort. Eventually, the Mines family grew, men came home from war, marriages happened in abundance, and new little Mines grandbabies came and grew and started school. Andy made straight A's but C's in deportment. Seems she talked too much and was out of turn and interruptive on report card day. Punishment was handed out appropriately, but Andy, 'Kitty Fragilistic' and Grandad slipped off for a well-deserved ice cream cone. No mention to anyone, of course.

Statistics tell us that those children, who were either raised or lived a few years with loving grandparents, and who had a 'village' of aunts and uncles to monitor behavior, be a sounding board, love and teach good values turned out to be responsible, loving, productive parents and grand-parents as well.

Chapter Eight
They Are Going To Build A What? You Mean Right Here In the Desert?

'Kitty Abbycue,' the intrepid guard feline, stood in front of the newly painted sign, 'The Monistary of St. Anthony - A Dwelling Place.' "The Brothers did good', he said. In the middle of the Chama River Canyon, with a backdrop of some of the most beautiful and magnificent scenery in the world. It will be an exciting day. A day of celebration because a new novice monk will be arriving. 'Kitty Abbycue,' thought to himself, this young man has already made a long journey to get this far. And I don't mean just in miles, the biggest journey of his new life is ahead of him and in an oasis in the desert.

'Kitty Abbycue' walked to the edge of the river to say a prayer for his safe journey and to reflect upon his own life in this very holy place. His friend, 'Kitty Odin' was just coming down for a drink after morning prayers with his Brothers, the nearly 30 monks in residence. He lay down near his friend. 'Kitty Abbycue' very quietly said, "Each new novice that comes to the Monastery of St. Anthony reminds me of the story my grandfather told me."

"It was Spring. Aelrod Wall, O.S.B., the foundry prior to the Monastery of Christ in the desert and several monks who observed the Benedictine life According to the Rule came to beautiful Chama Canyon. Witnessed firsthand the unbelievable formations, the cliffs and the softly flowing Chama River. It was deemed a perfect place to promote solitude and quiet for the cenobitic monastic life. In the Spring, Geronda Ephraim and others took a drive into the Sonoran desert. He wanted to look for a site for the St. Anthony's Monastery, and all of a sudden, church bells started ringing where no structure existed to have bells. The spirit gave Geronda Ephraim the exact place for the Cross to be placed as the foundation for the Monastery.

When the first monks came from Greece, they cleared the land in the heat of the summer. My grandfather met my grandmother that hot summer. Again, out of nowhere, a long-haired, white beauty from Persia. They lived in the refectory. This dining room always smelled good, and my grandfather always said the milk and the naps were awesome. , more monks arrived to help build the Monastery. All were young men monastic aspirants just like our young brother who will be coming today.

"In January, the Monastery celebrated the Feast of St. Anthony. My grandparents said it was wonderful even though the main church construction was not completed. Many pilgrims came to honor Saint Anthony. 'The first Abbot, who is our supreme spiritual leader, was enthroned, and then he tonsured all the new monks." 'Kitty Odis' asked his friend, "What's that?" "Oh, that's when he cuts the hair off the tops of their heads as a preparation for entering our religious order." "Well, I would say that was a day to remember, and in the desert!" grinned 'Kitty Odis.'

'Kitty Abbycue' said, "I think we need to get up to the entrance. Our newest novice brother should be arriving shortly."

"Welcome, Brother. Your Brothers in Christ are waiting for you in the sanctuary. We will then have evening prayers and a light dinner, and then you can retire. We feel blessed that your journey was an uneventful one." "Thank you, my brother, 'Kitty Abbycue.' I am the one who is most blessed."

Chapter Nine
Let's Just Respect The 'Bones' Of This Ole' House!

"Hey, 'Speedy,' knock it off!, shouted 'Kitty Bombay.' I know you were the caretaker of the grand old house for over twenty years, and you still are - only in a different way. But, for one day, would you not hang out on the staircase, lock the doors so guests can't get out, or do other antics and take that cigar outside? The end-of-year school trips start, and you might just scare the little guys and their teachers."

The Victorian house laughed at her favorite black cat with the black whiskers and the apparition that had lived as the resident ghost goes at it like brothers.

The house explained to 'Kitty Bombay' that ever since that day, her beloved caretaker was shot and killed, he still continued on as the caretaker. For over twenty years, he faithfully watched over us with the details of a military sergeant. Friend vowed to keep me and my grounds just as it was when I was built in 1895 for Dr. and Mrs. Rosson. He believed he was the caretaker of the grandest Queen Anne Victorian house ever built. I have to agree."

'Kitty Bombay' asked, "Why did the Rossons' come here?" If I understand it correctly, in 1879, Dr. Rosson left the Army as the Assistant surgeon and came to Phoenix, married Miss Flora Murray, and what a grand lady she was. though the intent was to set up a medical practice, which he did put in an office with all those awful looking tools on the first floor, over time, he became deeply involved with politics and even served as the Mayor." 'Kitty Bombay' said, "Well, I heard that didn't go very well, and not only did he resign before the end of his term, he sold out, took his wife and five children and moved out to California." "Yes, you are right."

The sun came in the parlor windows where the beautiful organ sat. Now, I'm just waiting for an occasional guest to play. When Dr. Rosson and his beautiful wife had me built on land actually purchased by Flora from a relative, it had a lot of 'firsts.' We continue, as do others, to enjoy my round moon gate and the French Octagonal Turret. Some say it is a one-of-a-kind house and refer to it as a 'haunted house,' bathrooms with running water, kitchen like no other intrigued all the future owners with a need for little change."

'Kitty Bombay' remarked, "You sure have taken on a lot of changes since the 'Doc' left. Did you meet 'Speedy'? Long story, he said. Dear Kai 'Speedy' Skounborg moved in with me long after the good Doctor had sold me and moved to L.A. 'Speedy' became a tenant when I became a boarding house. I admit, I liked it best when the Dr., his wife and children lived here. , 'Speedy' and I met and became great friends when he became the best caretaker in the West. He was a perfect entertainer, too, and always had a cigar in his mouth. I'm thinking more for chewing than smoking." "Oh, I remember when you were in a boarding house. Owners tore the place up, took the side porch, made it into another kitchen and added bathrooms. Speedy' was cleaning morning to night so nothing in the rooms would be damaged. Never heard a grumbling peep out of him, though." "Yes, the organ was played often, children danced in the parlor, women had afternoon tea, and those were good times, I have to say."

'Kitty Bombay' said, "One thing we all can agree, Mr. Petit, the Architect really knew what he was doing. The Rossons were waiting for him to design and build. They lived in a little adobe house. sure came a long way up the ladder!" Everyone laughed at that one.

"At the time, 'Speedy' was caretaker, and we went from a boarding house to a City-owned house/turned Museum. He continued to open the Museum each morning, kept the grounds with perfection and was a favorite tour guide for all who entered. After all, no one knew my every board better than 'Speedy.' He never closed me down until everything inside was 'ship-shape.' He had to move out of his upstairs room and move into a trailer out back. It was then someone took his life, and I lost my best friend, at least I thought I did. I should have known better."

'Kitty Bombay' and the grand old house, now renovated and alive again, believe their caretaker haunts the Museum. Visitors to the museum often see phantom sitings. He appears at will. Some have seen a silhouette or shadow and heard noises, especially on the staircase. Are mysteriously moved and then appear in place later. It is felt 'Speedy,' the beloved caretaker continues guarding 'the grand ole' gal, in an unpaid position, of course.

The Rosson House is one of Phoenix's architectural wonders and one of the oldest surviving houses in the City.

Having survived many owners and renters, The City of Phoenix is now the owner, and today, the house is a Museum for all to enjoy.

Chapter Ten

My Dad's a Haberdasher, and We Live Near the Monongahela River In a Little Red Brick House. No Wonder You Have a Funny Name.

'Kitty Bouncer' followed alongside Mr. Amochelas as they walked briskly to 'Amos' Store to work - just as they do every day, rain or shine. "We have a lot of produce coming in this morning. You need a keen eye today so those striker ruffians don't try to steal everything before I can get them on the shelves for sale. Know these are hard times, but stealing is stealing", said the conscientious Produce Manager. Amos already has most of the strikers' families on credit now anyway." 'Kitty Bouncer' agreed and added, "And those pesky mice seem to follow the produce trucks into the store. Maybe that's why they call me 'Kitty Mouser Bouncer'." Mr. 'A' smiled.

"'Mr. A', why don't you and your brothers work in the steel mill? They have a union, and my friend, 'Kitty Adara,' told me all of her master family has for generations worked at one of the Mills on the river."

'Mr A' looked down at his little, furry, feline friend and said, "Right now, we are nearing our workplace and must start our day. Produce needs to be unloaded, cleaned, marked and ready for sale. But, I promise, tonight I will try and tell you about 'The Why.'"

That evening 'Mr. A' and 'Kitty Mouser Bouncer' walked the same route home. A little slower, perhaps because it was a very long day. As they climbed what seemed like a hundred steps up to the little red brick house on 12th Avenue, a familiar smell of chicken soup with matza balls and tzimmes with a little leftover brisket that had been cooked all day, dutifully watched over by the family 'Bubbe.' It could be smelled before opening the front door. You can even smell the honey and cinnamon.

After dinner, as promised, 'Mr. A' pulled his friend up in the old and favorite after-dinner chair. "Good work today. Certainly lived up to your name, 'Kitty Bouncer'. It included the neighborhood ruffians and mice."

"Our grandparents and parents could tell this story better than me, but even though every detail or date may be off, I will give it a try. Many years ago, our Jewish families came to a free America. Place, unlike our old country where we were not protected. Did not come here like many European immigrants did to work in the Steel Mills. Early families settled here because many of us were Jewish farmers, and the beautiful rolling farmlands and the beautiful river, Called 'The Mon,' made it feel like a perfect place to build a community, a Jewish House of Worship, and develop the shops necessary for us to open up a business. We were and still are merchants and artisans. My grandfather was a farmer/later a grocer. Uncle Vinny was a Taylor and Haberdasher, and others owned the butcher shop and even saloon keepers."

"I liked your Uncle Tustaris. He always gave me little bits of meat at the butcher shop when I was really little." 'Kitty Bouncer' smiled, remembering the good times even his own father spoke of." "Yes, he was a kind soul and always was willing to help those who could not find work to feed their families."

"'Mr. A' continued, "As you see, I am a second-generation grocer and have no desire to do anything else. Especially work at any Mill on the river. We contributed to the life of the town and still do."

"My grandfather always talked about "Rivers of Steel." Meaning no matter where you worked, it was near a Mill on the river, and you did not live far either."

"What happened, asked 'Kitty Bouncer'?

The story goes that in July 1892, there was a huge disagreement between the workers in the union, who had been told their wages were going to be cut, not raised and Carnegie, the biggest owner of the steel factories. It turns out it got really bad, and the plant manager in charge shut the workers out of the factories. Then, all-you-know-what broke out into a violent mess. The plant manager not only shut them out for striking but hired at least 300 Pinkerton detectives to sneak up on barges to keep anyone from entering work. Strikers and their families exploded, and gunfire came from both sides. Killing at least twelve in a bloody fight that also injured many people. I was told that the strikers got everything from old antique guns to a cannon! Pinkerton finally gave up. Jews were not hired in the mills. We were not part of the strike as union or non-union workers. Did see soldiers go up our street, keeping peace for some time. Did not really want Grandpa going to work for fear of getting in the midst of the mess."

"Things got really bad. No work, bills were not paid, no money to buy food, make house payments, nothing! They suffered, we all suffered. There was a lot of blame to go around. Some blamed the Jews because no one in the factories would hire them, and it was spread around that they were retaliating. Just like how the start of the Glassworks factory changed everything from farming to industry, the Strike of 1892 had a profound effect. The Union quit giving strikers benefits and would not re-hire them. The Union stopped for many years. Times in the Mills always trickled down to us. We depended on the steel mills to continue giving jobs, which meant money back to the community. Kept our Jewish-owned businesses alive."

"Holy Cow, you sure have a good memory and quite a story to tell. I must say, this Jewish community has come a long way, remarked 'Kitty Bouncer.' Hesitated a moment and said, "Can I ask one more question?"

"Of course, replied 'Mr. A'. Well, my connections tell me Homestead was once known for **'steel and vice**.' Do you know how many bordellos were here?" asked 'Kitty Mouser Bouncer.'

"'Mrs. A' does not allow that kind of talk in or near this house. Neither of us will get any chicken soup with matza balls if she hears trash talk. Understood?" A meek reply. "Yes, Sir".

'Mr. A' said, "One last thing which is very important, and something you should always remember, 'Kitty Bouncer.' In May 1909, President Howard Taft visited Rodef Shalon. It was the first time in the country that a U.S. sitting President spoke from the pulpit of a Jewish House of Worship during regular Sabbath services. At Rabbi Levy's invitation, President Taft spoke briefly. Praised the Jewish people and said he wanted to be known as the President of ALL American people, and our government must be for ALL the people."

LATER that night.

"That's the best chicken soup with matza balls I have ever had. Mr A.'"

"My pleasure," said Mr. Amschalas, grinning from ear to ear.

Chapter Eleven
The Woman of This Ole' House Can Cook, Clean, Wash Clothes, and She's Gonna Vote!

It's 1848, and Marge Grayson seemed distracted this morning. Her list today was baking six pies for the church fundraiser for the Quaker Charities and sewing patches on the knees of the twins' blue jeans. Tyler and Taylor wore them out faster than she could find the time to fix them. But, the real list was the stack of papers slid into the secretary drawer in the parlor. Meetings had been going on in her parlor for months now in preparation for the first-ever Women's Rights Conference that is to be held in the Wesleyan Chapel in Seneca Falls, New York.

'Kitty White Claws' watched his nervous acting mistress, "What's all this craziness goin' on over women voting? Like you and your friends, Ms. Mott and Ms. Stanton might get into a bunch of trouble. parlor gets pretty loud with all those opinions floatin' around." Marge Grayson took off her kitchen apron and laid it neatly on the back of the kitchen chair. Six pies were cooling on the little pads and would be delivered to the church recreation hall later.

"'Kitty White Claws,' it is hard to explain, but what we want to get out of this National Convention is a referendum that will be similar to the Declaration of Independence that says "All men are created equal." Ours will be called 'The Declaration of Sentiments,' which will say, "All men and women are created equal." "You see, we are not allowed to vote or own property, and depending on location, religious beliefs, and numerous other 'can't do's.' want equal treatment under the law." 'Kitty White Claws' leaned up against his mistress and said, "Well, all I want is for you and those ladies to be careful. Now, there are black slaves who aren't allowed to do much of anything, including vote without permission from somebody and are even owned by someone else. Fact: I hear there is talk of a Civil War all over slavery. You can get hurt very easily." "Thank you, my little friend. Think we best get these pies down to the recreation hall."

The National Conference

'Kitty White Claws' pranced around among the long skirts of the dedicated women. "It's an exciting day. A much-awaited one. Many women have worked very hard. Twelve resolutions of the Declaration of Sentiments were signed by 68 women and 82 men, including Mr. Grayson. The resolutions set forth calling for equal treatment for women and men under the law AND voting rights for women. I think all those meetings in the Grayson house must have paid off." grinned the 'feline in charge.'

Weeks, months and even years rolled by. The Civil War ended, the formation of the American Equal Rights Association, the Ratification of the 14th Amendment, and the First National Women's Rights Convention with over 1,000 in attendance, and a former slave gave a spellbinding speech, "Ain't I a Woman!".

The twins grew up, graduated from college and, like their mother, were strong advocates for 'equal rights for all.'

'Kitty White Claws II' continued her feline family's support of women's rights. However, not everything went smoothly. Paul, a Quaker suffragist, fought every year for giving women the right to vote. She even authored the Equal Rights Amendment of 1923, but it was not ratified. Things had gotten worse. 'Kitty White Claws' watched 8,000 women march from the U.S. Capital to the White House the day before President-elect Woodrow Wilson was inaugurated. He was President, the Titanic sank, he declared war against Germany, and '2000' 'Silent Sentinels, ' all dressed in white, picketed the President's house and office for eighteen long months. did not speak but carried signs saying, "Mr. President, how long must a woman wait for liberty?" Some peaceful suffragettes numbering over 150 were arrested, beaten, harassed, and put in jail for 'obstruction of traffic' charges. Paul even went on a hunger strike. But they did not stop. There were conferences to draw attention, speeches, organizers and more years of hard work."

42 YEARS LATER

The 19th Amendment was passed by Congress on June 4, 1919, and ratified on August 18, 1920, guaranteeing all American women the right to vote. Years later..1923, the Equal Rights Amendment (E.R.A.) was proposed in Congress in an effort to secure equality for women.

President Woodrow Wilson had a full plate while serving as President of the United States, but I think he answered the 'Silent Sentinels' question, "How long must a woman wait for liberty?"

'Kitty White Claws II" said, "I think I heard him say, "TOO long!"

Chapter Twelve
Hello! Anyone Home?

'Kitty Klay' stood in awe. "You said we were going to visit your friend 'Clifty,' who lives in a rock house. You didn't say it was a big, ginormous cliff where people carved out a house to live." 'Kitty Kairo' laughed.

'Clifty' yelled, and it echoed across the canyon. "Hi 'Kitty Kairo'. It's been a lifetime since you last visited, and you brought a friend." 'Clifty,' this is 'Kitty Klay,' my very best friend. "Nice to see you both. It has been very quiet and lonely since the Basket Makers left."

"Why, this thing is a mile long. 'Clifty,' How did they get up so high anyway? Asked 'Kitty Kairo.' 'Clifty' said, "Well, the Basket Makers knew there were many predators out there. Not just animals but also other tribes and hunters. So, they started carving and carving, and the next thing I knew, you could hear women's voices as they made their beautiful baskets, babies were being born, religious rites were being held, and they could see anyone on high before they knew it. They carved it right, which would provide natural protection for hiding the cliff dwellers."

"What a nice rock house to live in said 'Kitty Klay' but parts of this look a little unfinished or something. It's so very beautiful, but the stonework looks like they just picked up and left. Did something happen, 'Crafty'? They put a lot of effort into building fireplaces, rooms, and holes cut to preserve food. Looks like a big stone city."

"Good questions, fellas. Over time, others came who were farmers. They worked the soil, and you could see the yellow flint corn for miles and miles. And they knew how to get water to the crops. People stayed with me through the long winter. You know, the quiet months when our outside world died, and they prayed for spring. I can say that those who came before the Basket Makers and after also left their mark. Always love the spring when the women would go pull the stringy fibers off the broad-leafed yucca. They work hours and hours making the men sandals and little shoes for their babies. They string the yucca into cords that they use for coats and nets. "

'Clifty' remembering back, said, "I often never knew what their tribal name was. I do know that they brought their own special talents and gifts into my dwelling. Even left their craft behind. Left without warning, never to be seen again."

'Kitty Kairo' said, "You mean they just like melted into the air?" 'Kitty Klay' laughed. 'Clifty,' do you think they may have left their ghosts in your rocks?" He replied, "Well when the wind blows just right, I think so. I'm going to say, 'thank you' for letting us stay awhile in the safety of your dwelling."

"Fellas, I hope you will come back and often. Never know when a new family will move in."

As the sun began to set on the old cliff dwellings, 'Kitty Klay' and 'Kitty Kairo' waved goodbye to their friend.

'Until next time!'

Chapter Thirteen
A Forever Home For Charlie!

'Kitty Fondley' gathered his five feline friends together for an important meeting. The 72 covered wagons that are home to 300 emigrants left Missouri for a new life at the end of the Oregon Trail and are circling for a two-day rest. Humans and stock need a rest. 2,000-mile trek along the Oregon Trail has already proven to be exhausting, dangerous and deadly. What are we going to do? Asked 'Kitty Lakin'. Five babies have lost their mamas during the measles outbreak. The Indian raids have left at least ten children that we know of without either parent. And it grows each day!"

'Kitty Fondley' shook his head and, with a sad reply, said, "Well, they are hoping to get them adopted along the way." 'Kitty Larkin' jumped up and said, "And just where is 'along the way'? Families are gonna jump out of the trees in ten feet of snow?"

'Kitty LaRuse,' a long-haired white Persian asked, "How can we help? Right now, it looks like first things first. I think, for starters, we need to go easy on the milk. These babies must have milk to survive. We can drink less." All agreed.

"Okay, each of us will go to a covered wagon where there is a newborn. Remember, if they get cold, they will die. Up and cover them like a blanket and sing. Yes, sing just like their mama might do. It calms them down." *Everyone volunteered for the job.*

Mrs. Norma Bradford, a Catholic missionary who is headed to the next Fort with the wagon train, has volunteered to gather as much milk as can be spared for the babies from the numerous cows belonging to emigrants and is circulating a letter to each and every wagon with an adoption plea.

'Kitty Fondley' called her feline volunteers. "We are hearing from the scouts, who just returned, that there are rumblings of more Indian raidings on wagon trains. The Snake Indians, known for their speed, dangerous behavior and lightning-like strikes, are in front of us. They are very angry. Don't care that half this wagon train is going for free land. Free because of the Donation Land Claim Act, designed to promote homesteading. 320 acres per man and another 320 if he has a wife."

'Kitty Lakin' replied, "Yes, I am told that it all sounded good, but no one told them that the wagon trains were going to bring measles cholera and that they would kill more buffalo along the way than was needed and left dead animals all over. , the railroad expansion, and mining for gold and silver, which polluted the very springs they needed to survive. ALL on land that does not belong to the white man. Their women and babies are dying of starvation, and revenge is rampant."

'Kitty Fondley' said, "Glory be! At 640 acres each, it does not take long to take up a lot of land. I can see where they see all these missionaries, land speculators, gold developers and just those immigrants wanting a new life could leave little land for any Indian Tribe to live, farm, hunt and raise their own families."

Mrs. Bradley has decided to address the adoption of the five babies and ten other children. She is holding a fireside meeting to discuss the wagon train dilemma. Protestant families did not want to adopt catholic babies even if Mrs. Bradley was a Catholic missionary.

'Kitty LaRuse' said, "Look out. She's getting up on her soap box, and in about a minute, "she will cloud up and rain all over everybody." All the feline baby volunteers remarked that the babies would, no doubt, be the easiest to adopt. The others, especially 'Charlie,' may not be so easily placed."

'Kitty Fondley' said, "Charlie is so special. No one knows much about his parents. They rarely strayed away from their covered wagon, which was mostly destroyed in the last raid. Though Charlie does not speak, does not look or act like other children, he smiles from ear to ear. He was found sitting on the ground next to his parents. His little hands clutched the family Bible. Cayuse Tribe are constantly on the move, and they believe all the land belongs to them. They even go to war with other tribes along the Oregon Trail. A tribe is made up of a lot of young warriors who all want to be The Chief one day. They just happened to have found dead buffalo and the loss of animal skin they needed to survive, and that's all it took. Charlie's parents were in the wrong place that day.

Wagonmaster, 'Mr. Milt' saw 'Charlie with his Bible, scooped him up and hid him in the heavily guarded ammunition wagon. Never moved. Kitty Koragious', the elder on the wagon train, has taken over watching 'Charlie' and makes sure he is fed and dry. She has been with 'Mr. Milt' since being abandoned at birth. Most days, she is seen either walking beside 'Charlie' or on a pillow beside him.

The End of the Road

Forty of the seventy-two covered wagons survived the trip. Disease, accidents, outlaws, and less frequent but deadly Indian raids all contributed to the loss of men, women and children. Babies were adopted. All Catholic missionaries on the trip felt it their 'divine' calling (according to Mrs. Bradley) to make a Christian life for nine of the children. The twins were adopted by the Faulkners, who had no children. Since they will be starting a new church, all children should stay together. All that is except 'Charlie.

Wagonmaster 'Milt' and his wife, Martha, decided to adopt a little baby girl, and they named her 'Charity,' her new little brother 'Charlie.' Wagonmaster Milt retired at the end of the trial. 'Kitty Koragious' can still be seen walking along with 'Charlie' and 'Charity,' who now have a village to help look out after them.

'Charlie' has a lot to smile about these days.

Chapter Fourteen

The White House Is Different Because It Is The Grandest House Of ALL!

The majestic 'President's House,' also known as the 'People's House' built around 1800, watched his faithful companions, who had lived and served him for the past thirty-four years. They were just waking up from a short night's sleep.

"Well, good morning, 'Kitty Roxy'. We both seem to be getting slower at moving around these days." "Yes, Sir, I do believe so. I think you have held up marvelously well since the day our first resident president, John Adams, moved in. It is still the people's living space. Those Brits did a number on the Executive residence, but your remodel, which tried to put you back like new, took some time."

"I remember well the time you and 'Mr. B,' the new pantry keeper, started as part of the new White House staff. You had to live in Blair House with President Truman until the floor in the President's quarters was complete. The staff was so nervous because the new president, who was once the vice president, was coming in."

'Kitty Roxy' laughed. "We were all shocked to look up to see President Truman, the 33rd U.S. President, standing in the kitchen." "Good morning. Could I have a pot of tea for Mrs. Truman, please?" "This was our first interaction with ANY President, and he was standing outside the pantry door!"

"Looking back, 'Kitty Roxy,' you and many others must have wondered what Mr. Truman might do about that A-Bomb. We now know it sure ended the war. The whole world took notice! 'Mr. B' liked him. He told me that this President stood up for our black brothers in the military. President Truman had a lot of famous sayings, but when he said that if they were going to fight and die for us, then they should have equal rights," He got our vote. 'W.H.' said, "Don't forget his famous quote -"If you can't stand the heat - get out of the kitchen!"

"I always wondered when he slept."

Another moving day.

'W.H.' said, "Get ready for a change!" 'Kitty Roxy' said to 'Mr. B', "Have you ever seen so many badges, medals, and stars on one uniform? I felt like I needed to stand at attention all the time. I really liked First Lady 'Mamie Eisenhower' though. She smiled all the time. 'W.H.' said that President Eisenhower was very different from President Truman. He sent Civil Rights legislation that got the Civil Rights Act of 1957 enacted *and* signed the Civil Rights Act of 1960 into law!" 'Kitty Roxy' frowned and said, "Well, I remember those darn squirrels running all over your lawn. I was in charge, and I can't tell you how many times I got chased instead of the other way around. *And* all because those pests messed up President Ike's golf game! Our 5-Star, West Point graduate from Abilene, Kansas, did well."

Reminiscing, 'W.H.' said, "Didn't you just love those early

years when John F. Kennedy became the 35th U.S. President? My walls rang with voices of children running through my halls. 'Kitty Roxy' smiled. "That little girl, Caroline and her little brother John-John, they called him, always made my day. 'Mr. B' would come up from the kitchen, delivering a tray of milk and cookies. Earlier, he delivered the President's breakfast tray of orange juice, poached eggs on toast, crisp broiled bacon, marmalade, milk and coffee, and I loved any bits he might share. The minute they heard 'Mr. B' coming into the Oval Office, they scampered out from beneath the President's desk where they often played. Sometimes, little Caroline would scoop me up, and we would go watch a James Bond movie with the President. I loved those days."

A dark day in America and around the world.

'Kitty Roxy' and her friend, 'Mr. B' were in the kitchen when people started screaming. 'W.H.' doors were banging in all 132 rooms. Downstairs and upstairs and in the residence. Since President and Mrs. Jackie Kennedy were in Dallas, Texas, to support the upcoming candidates, everyone was scrambling to get accurate information. Limousines by the dozens started coming into my driveway. Secret service men were overwhelmed by the lack of news.

"Our President has been assassinated." Mrs. Kennedy is okay.

Not a dry eye in the house and across the world. Flags immediately lowered. 'W.H.' gathered all staff. "We must prepare for our quick goodbyes and set the kitchen in motion for many cabinet members and numerous dignitaries. Hot water for tea, coffee and trays of sweets and savories. And, of course, we will be available to First Lady Jackie Kennedy and the children for whatever they need. Remember, this is her house too!"

"A new President will be here soon. President Lynden B. Johnson has already been sworn in on Air Force One. Our entire staff will be working tirelessly to make sure each and every person who walks through the door is treated with dignity. 'Mr. B' got an invitation to the funeral. He declined, saying, "I need to be here to serve all who come through this great house.

A Dark Day Indeed!!

Everything is quiet... No little voices. "Hard to believe 'Kitty Roxy' that it is 1963, and a new family is moving in. 'W.H.' tried to explain that a 'Lady Bird' was moving in, but it was President Johnson's wife's nickname. Not one in a cage." "Well, that's a relief," said, 'Kitty Roxy.'

President Johnson,' L.B.J.,' he was called, championed Civil Rights again, which made 'Mr. B', the Butler happy. "He sure bellowed racial profanities at times, but he signed The Voting Rights Act of 1965 and the Social Security Amendment of 1965. More than once, 'Mr. B' took a little warm milk and scotch in to help L.B.J. relax a little..' W.H.' grinned.

"'W.H.,' 'Mr.B,' what in the world are all those trucks coming in the gate?" yelled 'Kitty Roxy.' "Oh, that's the First Lady 'Lady

Bird's beautification program for America. She's all about cleaner water, cleaner air, and clean highways. You will see a lot of changes over the next few months, I am told." said 'W.H..'

"Wow, have you ever seen so much color? Beautiful colored flowers everywhere. Gorgeous daffodils and azaleas along Pennsylvania Avenue. The dogwood and cherry trees will grow big, and in the spring, my oh! My, what a sight for visitors," an excited feline told his friends.

Ms. Lady Bird' said, "Where flowers bloom, so does hope."

Ms. Lady Bird Johnson earned the Presidential Medal of Freedom in 1977 and the Congressional Gold Medal in 1984 for her tireless efforts in the beautification of America.

President Lyndon B. Johnson, our U.S. 36th President, sadly left this House in 1969. The Vietnam War negatively impacted us all - including the President of the United States.

It's 1969, a moving day for a new President *again.* Richard M. Nixon and his wife, Pat. 'Kitty Roxy' looked at W.H. and asked, "How many men do you know who were defeated for President, defeated for Governor, and lived in the Vice president's house and now here in the 'W.H.' as well." 'W.H.' thought a moment, then said, "Certainly none that I can recollect. I do know, 'Kitty Roxy,' that Richard Nixon wanted to be an FBI agent. He didn't get a callback, so heck, he might as well run again for President!" Laughs could be heard all the way through the downstairs.

"I dearly loved to wake up early morning, and as the staff prepared for the happenings of the day, you could hear President Nixon playing the baby grand piano. You thought you were sitting with a concert pianist at the Kennedy Center. Just marvelous." smiled W.H.H.

"Wow, what is going on? I don't know about you, W.H.H., but I have never seen so much art coming through the front door. The workers said at least 600 pieces." 'Mr. B', the house Butler, said, "Well, fellas, we got 132 rooms and 35 bathrooms. I'm thinking they can find some space to hang them. First Lady Pat Nixon was a Personal Representative of the President. A personable and gracious First Lady. We will remember her fondly."

Another dark day in the 'House.'

August 8, 1974, 'W.H.,' 'Kitty Roxy,' and 'Mr. B' reached the Oval Office, where T.V. cameras, the Press and human traffic ran into each other. The President is about ready to address the American people.

President Nixon, the 37th U.S. President, has resigned.

"Strange things continue to happen in the big White House said, 'Kitty Roxy.' Gerald R. Ford, Jr., who had served as vice president and is now the 38th U.S. President, was never elected either.

'W.H.' said, "We have to remember he did have some extraordinary circumstances with, you know, Nixon's resignation and all. Not too many Presidents give a full pardon to their predecessor."

"President Ford's wife, Betty, was not well during most of the 895 days they were with us. She became an advocate for cancer awareness and Equal Rights. She handled it all with dignity and grace."

'Mr. B' came through with a tray for President Ford and said, 'Kitty Roxy.' do you know our President was a star college football player *and* could have played for the Detroit Lions and the Green Bay Packers? Really? Oh, 'Mr. B,' you are wanted in the First Lady's private sitting room. She requested a small cake with your coffee tray. It is President Ford's birthday, and 'Ms. Betty wants to sing him Happy Birthday." 'Mr. B' smiled. As they opened the door to let everyone into the private sitting room, everyone started singing 'HAPPY BIRTHDAY,' not to President Ford, but to 'Mr. B,' the Butler, who shared a birthday.

The First Lady proceeded to cut the cake for her husband, a faithful Butler and family.

"Good Morning, President Carter." The White House and staff welcomed the 39th U.S. President and the First Lady, Rosalyn Carter. It's 1977. 'Mr. B', the Butler said, "Welcome, Sir, you sure have a lot on your plate. May I get you something? "No sir, I will get my own. Don't need to wait for me. The First Lady would like her office in the *East* wing outfitted as soon as possible. First Lady Rosalynn Carter will be my personal emissary to Latin America. She has numerous projects and interests. Thank you for supporting her. I'll find my way to the kitchen when I'm hungry. 'Mr. B' said, "Sir, would you like a dinner menu?" "Oh, that won't be necessary. We'll eat whatever you eat." 'Kitty Roxy' stood quietly and then whispered, "Huh, what do we eat? Is that what he said?" The Georgia Plains-born peanut farmer with a devotion to the Baptist faith saw little reason to have waited on hand and foot. Efficiency in government and the removal of racial barriers were of utmost importance.

The 'W.H.' later remarked that things were rough in those years with the taking of American captives and high inflation, among other political events. It sort of overshadowed all the really good things, like creating the Department of Education and Civil Service Reform. The Soviet invasion of Afghanistan did not help any.

A good thing - the 53 Americans held hostage were released on the same day President Carter left office.

The moving truck arrived on schedule.

Oh! Those Reagon years!

*"W.H., we got a movie actor and a movie actress moving into the White House!" "I mean a **real** movie actor, squealed 'Kitty Roxy.' "OK, OK, 'W.H.' said, but today he is moving into MY house, and he is Ronald Reagan, the 40th U.S. President. His wife, Nancy, was a First Lady before. First Lady of California. Very impressive*

background. In fact, she is going to kick off her 'Just Say No' drug awareness campaign.

"It sure seems as though President Reagan runs circles around everybody. One minute, he is meeting on a big build-up of our military, then a group talking about technology development for missile defense systems and Grenada boy, that's a big one.", said 'Kitty Roxy.'

The President has been shot!!

"Oh no! A very upset 'W.H.' yelled. Not again. He has only been in office for 69 days! Being rushed to the hospital. The First Lady is on her way."

Welcome home, Mr. President. We are grateful to hear our dear friend, James Brady is improving, and the wounded policemen and Secret Service are being cared for.

'Mr. B' said, "We want to follow the diet both the Dr. and the First Lady have requested. **But I want all candy jars full of Mr. President's favorite jelly beans. Understood? Yes. Sir.**

"Whether you liked him or not, 'W.H.,' he was credited with a peaceful end to the Cold War and was ranked in the upper tier of all Presidents." remarked 'Kitty Roxy.' "Yes, 'Mr. B chimed in. The First Lady was an author and wrote about the Foster Grandparent Program. **And** I'll never forget the day we hosted First Ladies from 17 countries for a conference on 'Saying No' to drugs and alcohol. That drove the Secret Service into a frenzy. But they all ate good."

"You got that right!"

It is January, 1989. What a long and wonderful ride, Mr. White House. For over thirty years and eight Presidents, we have served together. We all believe that Ronald Reagan, the 40th President of the United States, restored faith in the American Dream. 'Kitty Roxy' and I will be retiring with The Reagans. 'Mr. B' said, "Who would have thought that I would go from a pantry man from a plantation to the Maitre d' of the most important House in America? We grew up with segregation and likely will see a black man elected to your White House."

"The moving trucks are arriving. They have a short trip. Vice-President George H.W. Bush will be moving in. A new member of staff will soon welcome them. And look who is here. 'Kitty Dutch' ", said 'Kitty Roxy'. "Best get on your running shoes, my friend.

Goodbye, my friends. God Bless you, and God Bless America.